Thinking of You

DONNA TURNBULL

Published in Australia in 2022

© 2022 Donna Turnbull. All Rights Reserved. Except for brief excerpts for review purposes, no part of this book may be reproduced or used in any form without written permission from the publisher.

All Scripture is taken from the Holy Bible, New International Version®, NIV® Copyright ©1973, 1978, 1984, 2011 by Biblica, Inc.® Used by permission. All rights reserved worldwide.

Paperback ISBN: 978-0-646-86389-4

Subjects: Religion / Christian Living / Devotional / Inspirational

DONNA TURNBULL is the only daughter of loving parents. Throughout her childhood she developed a desire to do what was right and true. At the same time, she was often in a world of her own. This helped her to develop her imagination, but she also nurtured some very self-centred attitudes. It wasn't until her late teens that she became painfully aware of her shortcomings and sought to find answers to the big questions of life. These included: "Is God real?"; "Can someone believe in God and not be a Christian?"; and "How does Jesus fit in?". Soon after her eighteenth birthday she wanted to get right with God and that was the turning point of her life. She began a lifelong friendship with God, which led her on many adventures. One such adventure took her to the Bible College of Queensland, where she explored all manner of questions. Another part of her journey was through the highways and byways of Australia and New Zealand with a Christian drama ministry. As a qualified teacher and volunteer Christian instructor, she has developed the art of storytelling. Her favourite story to tell is about her best friend, her Lifesaver.

Contents

1. Gardening Glee 1
2. Laughter 5
3. Tell Me The truth 9
4. Grrr 12
5. The Battler 16
6. How Very Noble 19
7. Adventure 22
8. Appreciation 25
9. Interdependence Day 29
10. Two Men And Their Donkeys 33
11. Light 36
12. It's Not Fair 40
13. Whatever It Takes 43
14. Signs 47
15. Burdens 50
16. Video Chat With God 53
17. Easter Re-enactment 56

18 « Hail 59

19 « Pure Gold 62

20 « Who Is This Guy? 66

21 « Noble Service 70

22 « The Return 74

23 « Complaints Or Compliments 78

24 « Climbing The Ladder 81

25 « The Lifesaver 84

26 « Greatness 87

27 « The Ransom 91

28 « Will It Ever End? 94

29 « The Good Neighbour 97

30 « The Royal Wedding 101

31 « Citizenship 105

A note to the reader 108

Acknowledgements 110

1

Gardening Glee

A little boy wanted to help in the garden. He'd seen where Daddy kept his seeds and tools, so one afternoon he ran down to the shed and grabbed what he needed. He wanted to grow corn so he could have popcorn for family movie time, cornflakes for breakfast, and corn on the cob smothered with butter every night for dinner.

As he was walking along, he put some seeds on his hand, but with such a tiny fist, some of the seeds fell on the path. Seconds later there was a rustle of wings as two galahs competed to get the tasty seeds. Startled, the little boy started to run towards the back of the shed.

He crouched down in the shadow of the shed, hoping those noisy birds wouldn't be able to see him. The gravel crunched under his feet as his little feet got restless. To get up he needed both hands, so he let go his fist-full of seeds. They fell in amongst the gravel and the little boy pulled out another fist-full of the seeds.

Still afraid of the galahs, the boy crept through the long grass and weeds behind the shed. "Owwwww!" he cried, as a thistle brushed against his leg. Dropping his precious seeds he grabbed his leg, hopping up and down.

Hearing her little boy cry, Mum came rushing

down to the backyard. Seeing his tears, she scooped him up in a big cuddle and kissed it better. When the tears had dried up, the boy squirmed to get down. He took another fist-full of seeds and marched out towards the veggie patch. He was about to throw the seeds to the wind when Mum came and showed him how to plant them to grow the best popcorn plants ever.

Days passed until the toddler went to play with his bulldozer in the gravel. "Mummy, Mummy they growed!" he shouted excitedly. Sure enough, when his mum came to see, she saw a few tiny seedlings just poking their heads out of the gravel, the thistles, and the veggie patch.

By the end of the week, they were growing bit by bit, and each morning the little tyke eagerly ran down to see if any popcorn had grown. "Where'd they go?" the little boy asked as he searched frantically for his seedlings in the gravel. In their place there were wilted bits of stem. The lad ran to the thistles where he found a thistle had squeezed the life out of another tiny plant. Desperately he ran to the veggie patch where his precious plants were still growing. The boy poured rainwater from the tank into his watering can and drizzled water on these tender living things.

Day after day he lovingly nurtured the corn plants

until, "Mummy, Mummy! They growed ears!!" Sure enough, the corn crop was ready and that night at the dinner table a buttery grin munched happily on his corn on the cob. Secretly he planned to plant some of the corn kernels so he'd have more and more corn coming out his ears.

―·―

"Whoever has ears to hear, let them hear" (Mark 4:9).

Further reading: Mark 4:1-20

Prayer: *God, please sow good news into my life. Help me to listen, to grow in understanding and to be fruitful with what you sow into my life.*
Amen

2

Laughter

Is laughter truly a tonic? I am not a doctor, but I always feel better after a good belly laugh.

I once did a class in laughing. It was hilarious. We students all laid down on our backs and laughed. At first, we were a bit inhibited, but we soon got the hang of laughing using "hohoho" or "hahaha" or "heeheehee" or some other utterance. It was a good internal jogging session. I have since tried to convince others that I could lead a laughing class, but they have always been too inhibited. Sometimes I just go up to people and laugh. It usually makes them smile, or else they 'catch' the laughing bug and burst out laughing themselves.

Doing zany things can cause much laughter and tears of joy. I got creative and organised a 'bush walk' for my elderly parents. I hid plastic animals around the garden and acted as a tour guide, introducing the different animal habitats. My 'tour company' also offered a 'picnic lunch', which we ate at the kitchen table. One tourist had damper (toast) and vegemite with billy tea (tea made from water in the billy - the kettle) in an enamel mug. The whole experience was just so zany for adults to participate in, that it caused uninhibited laughter.

Telling stories can also cause much hilarity. Swapping stories of funny occurrences has had me in tears laughing. Street sign incidents have too. One that tickled my funny bone was a sign that said, 'Slow School'. Imagine a school moving slowly across the road! At the time, however, the school was moving so slowly that it had actually come to a complete stop! It's a good thing... it would've caused a major traffic jam at peak hour. Maybe it only moved slowly at night... a nocturnal wanderer!

I don't think laughter should ever be at someone, or at someone else's expense. Nor do I like crude jokes. Sarcasm has been described as the lowest form of wit too. Some cues for laughter cross over the line as people get hurt or degraded. That was never what laughter was intended for. Good belly laughs can come without showing disrespect for anyone.

"A cheerful heart is good medicine,
but a crushed spirit dries up the bones"
(Proverbs 17:22).

Further Reading: Proverbs 17

Prayer: *Loving God, thank you for giving us the ability to laugh and even cry with laughter. Forgive us for times that we have laughed at others or not treated others with dignity. Please help us to see the funny side of life and to enjoy the good medicine of a joyful heart. Amen*

3

Tell Me The Truth!

Surprise! Politicians don't always have the answers... sometimes they have more questions than we think. A famous politician asked an important question once. His question was "What is truth?" (John 18:38). It's a good question that many people have sought the answer to. What indeed is truth? How do we know if something is true or not?

When I was a child, my parents taught me that honesty is the best policy. I am grateful that they instilled this value into me in my formative years. I remember occasions where I was given too much change or was undercharged, and I felt compelled to tell the truth to the shop assistant. It cost me money, but it was a small price to pay to keep my integrity. I feel sorry for the kids who are trained by their parents to shoplift or lie. How are those kids supposed to know they should tell the truth? Where is their moral compass? How are the adults around them supposed to tell when the kids are telling the truth?

What is the nature of truth? There are some 'facts' that we agree on as conventions. For example, people all over the world would agree that 1+1=2 or that Canberra is the capital of Australia. We could mark them as 'true' in a true or false quiz. Then there are events that can be viewed from different points of view. There was much controversy over the Vietnam

War, for instance. What was true about that? Another kind of truth involves personal reflection. Is there even a fourth kind of truth... an objective truth that exists even if no one knows about it?

What is true then? It is true that I am alive, breathing, and pumping blood around my body. That's a physical truth. Emotionally I can experience different feelings. My feelings change and are fairly unreliable in determining what is true. Psychologically, I have a brain that is complex and sometimes goes into denial. Intellectually, I can see that what I observe with my senses is usually true but can be misleading. Spiritually, what is truth? That is the $64 million dollar question.

Further Reading: John 18:28-40

*Prayer: God, you know all things.
Help me to know what is true.
Amen*

4

Grrrr!

*G***rrrr!** Some old folk sound like bears, growling and getting grumpy. I am sure glad I don't know too many grumpy old men, or women for that matter. I don't want to grow to become one either. I don't want to be known as a crotchety old dame that complains and grumbles all the time or who never has a good word to say about anything. I don't want to be the grump who delights in complaining about every little detail... including how her tea is made. When I grow up and old, I want to be much more pleasant in my disposition than that.

I think I understand a little of why grumpy old folk become grumpy. As I grow older my body seems to be developing more and more aches and pains and sometimes it feels like I hurt all over. There are also emotional scars that twinge if someone hits that spot. Circumstances aren't always ideal in the world around me either and watching the news can be downright depressing. If I continually focus on the bad and ugly sides of life, I can get pretty grumpy.

At other times life can feel like a roller coaster... up and down. When circumstances are good, then I can be chipper, but when circumstances are not so good I can turn gloomy and glum. I can't always change the circumstances, but I can aim to respond to them gracefully. Instead of considering whether the glass is half full or half empty, I can seek to have the glass refilled.

I want to replace Grrrumpiness with Gratitude. There are so many things to be grateful for that it's impossible to count them. We live on a planet that has an atmosphere with air in it. We can be thankful each day that we wake up breathing in air. Our earth is just the right distance from the sun, so that we neither fry nor freeze. That means we can be thankful for our place in the solar system. Pure, liquid water can only be found on earth, so we can have gratitude that we don't live on Mars or other such environments that don't sustain life.

Having an attitude of gratitude isn't always easy and I don't always get it right, but each day is a new day to seek to focus on what is good.

"Finally, brothers and sisters, whatever is true, whatever is noble, whatever is right, whatever is pure, whatever is lovely, whatever is admirable—if anything is excellent or praiseworthy—think about such things" (Philippians 4:8).

Further Reading: Psalm 145

Prayer: *God you are so big and awesome. Thanks for the air I breathe. Thanks for our place in space. Thanks for water to drink and for life itself. Lord you are lovely, excellent and worthy of all praise. Thank you for your love and care. I admire your greatness and your ability to hold all things together.*
Amen

5

The Battler

She was a battler and just as well. The battles that she had were a tad overwhelming. Ruth was contemplating a life that was so different from what she was used to. The choice she had was between sinking into despair or moving to another country to resist the tide of disasters in her life.

Facing her husband's illness was an experience she would rather not have gone through. When her husband died, the pain was almost too much to bear. Then her mother-in-law announced that she was going back to the place she grew up in and encouraged Ruth to leave her.

To Ruth, that was unthinkable. "Ruth replied, 'Don't urge me to leave you or to turn back from you. Where you go I will go, and where you stay I will stay. Your people will be my people and your God my God'" (Ruth 1:16). She decided to trust her future into the hands of God.

True to her word, Ruth accompanied her mother-in-law to this country, so new to her, and began battling her way through poverty. She worked her fingers to the bone to provide for her mother-in-law. As the sun beat down, she picked up grain dropped by harvesters. It was back-breaking work, but she never complained.

Although she worked long hours and put some food

on the table, it wasn't enough. These two women were so poor. No amount of effort, however admirable, would ever be enough. They would never be able to work their way out of their poverty. They needed a gallant hero to rescue them from their situation.

A gentle, compassionate landowner stepped up to the mark. At first he provided a job, food and water, and a safe place to be. He helped them through the legal red tape and talked through what they needed to know. By the grace of God, he gently lifted these two destitute ladies out of the mire. When their own efforts fell short of the mark, he stepped in and saved the day.

Further Reading: Ruth

Prayer: *Thank you, God, for providing so many good things for me. Thank you that you do so much to help me in my difficulties. You are awesome. Please help me when circumstances seem overwhelming. Thank you for your loving kindness.*
Amen

6

How Very Noble!

What's the difference between a cab driver and a royal chauffeur? This is no joke, so there is no punch line, but the answer probably has to do with who the passengers are. The Royal Family are nobles, but is it possible for ordinary people to be noble? What does noble even mean? When I was in primary school the national anthem was about God saving the noble Queen. Was she noble because she was born into the Royal Family or because of a character trait that she showed? Personally, I think it's a combination of the two.

As a child I wanted to impress the Queen. To me, she was the epitome of nobility, and I wanted everything to be perfect for her. I made sure that the kitchen cupboards were perfectly tidy, because one day the Queen might come to tea and inspect them! Of course, that was ludicrous. The Queen was far too important to even enter my humble home, much less the kitchen. She was born a noble with 'blue' blood in her veins.

Over and over again the head of the British Empire had to make choices between personal preference and the crown. She sacrificed time, pleasure, and popularity with her family for the greater good. She chose to follow the noble route of denying her own desires for honourable intentions. While she was born into royalty, her character also showed nobility.

Not all people with royal bloodlines have demonstrated nobility. Past Kings and Queens have not always shown honour. Instead, they have grown autocratic with power, bloodthirsty with greed, blind with lust, misguided with pride or haughty with position. These qualities, while present in the best of us, are the opposite of nobility.

One man had the privilege of being married to the Queen - a rare noble. "A wife of noble character who can find? She is worth far more than rubies" (Proverbs 31:10). There is a Sovereign who inspires nobility in Kings and Queens, Princes, Princesses and Paupers. It's a quality that doesn't come naturally, but it is a beautiful trait, no matter what station in life one finds themselves in.

Further Reading: Philippians 4:5-8

Prayer: *God you are exceedingly noble. Please help me to look to your example to inspire honourable actions and attitudes.* Amen

7
Adventure

"I can't reach!" My little legs stretched from one stepping-stone to another, but it seemed like bridging an ocean. I couldn't do it on my own, but Dad was there. He was already way out in front, but when he saw that I was having trouble, he backtracked and reached out his steady arm. The creek still gurgled, and the rocks were still a stretch, but I trusted my strong daddy to help me across the divide. With his help I leapt from one rock to another as we gambolled along in the creek. He didn't have the adventure instead of me, but he was close enough that we had the adventure together. Dad didn't take away the challenges, but he made it possible to surmount them without falling. And he was close by if I did start to waiver.

God is not some far-off deity watching from a distant place. He dwells among us in the ordinary, challenging lives that we have, and He is not passive. He doesn't sit back in His rocking chair gazing dotingly on His children. Instead, He is an active presence who makes a difference, and He takes great delight in His kids. When we're afraid, He offers His strong support. If we feel like something is just too much of a stretch, He is there to help. He doesn't necessarily remove the obstacles, but He assists us to make leaps of faith. And He is with us in the adventures.

One day God is going to make all things even better than they are now. In the future there will be no tears, pain, or death. Funeral directors will need to find different jobs and so will medical specialists. There won't be any banged knees from falling on the rocks or torn muscles from over-stretching. People probably won't even have to write risk assessments. Now that's a pain we can do without! Our God is so awesome in power that He can recreate everything.

In the meantime, how are we helping others to see this rugged, adventurous God who dwells among us? He sets up camp with us and hikes the trails where we walk. Christianity is not for wimps. It's for the bold who are willing to take on the challenge of reaching out for the strong arm of the Lord and trusting that He can enable us to do the impossible.

Further Reading: Revelation 21:1-6

Prayer: *Strong and mighty God, thank you for being with me on this adventure called life. Thank you for being beside me in the challenges and for being trustworthy.*
Amen

8

Appreciation

There was a knock at the door. Mary, Martha, and Lazarus had invited a VIP to dinner. Was it him? These three siblings had a lot to thank him for. They had spent time together on other occasions, and they had a strong relationship. They were hosting a dinner party for their friend, to honour him and show their appreciation.

Lazarus honoured his guest by reclining at the table with him. He gave his guest of honour the gift of time. We don't know all of their conversation, but we know that Lazarus was with him. Did Lazarus express his thanks for all the kind things the guy had done? Did he honour the man by being an attentive listener? Did he show his appreciation by laughing and joking with his valued guest? Maybe they discussed matters of grave importance, or Lazarus could have been the life of the party to help his VIP to feel welcome.

Martha showed their family friend her appreciation by serving the dinner. She was a very practical person and it would appear that she knew how to organise a dinner party. On a prior occasion she had found out that listening to her guest of honour was more important than getting stuff done, so this time she didn't plead for help. What did she do instead? Did she greet their esteemed companion at the door with a smile? Did she serve the meal with delight? Was her attitude in serving one of generosity and gratitude for the opportunity to show appreciation to her friend?

Mary honoured their VIP with appropriate touch and lavish giving. Her gift was expensive. She gave profusely to express the overflow of her heart. Her appreciation was so deep that she would use something so precious to honour the one whom she loved as a dear brother. The cost to her was high, but it was worth it. Her gift, while being expensive, had more sentimental and symbolic value. Her friend was honoured.

The whole purpose of the gathering was to celebrate and honour one man. Having a friendship with this bloke had changed their lives and they were grateful to him. Their guest of honour was Jesus of Nazareth, and they wanted to show Him how appreciative they were.

Further Reading: John 12:1-8

Prayer: *Jesus, you showed that you were a good friend to Mary, Martha, and Lazarus. Thank you for all the kind things you have done for me too. Thanks for always being there and for being available to listen. Thanks for all that you do and all that you have given me. I appreciate it.*
Amen

9

Interdependence Day

Many countries celebrate their Independence Day, but I wonder if we've missed the point.

Many years ago, a young lady, Esther, and her older cousin were living in a country not their own, under oppression from a foreign power. Esther's parents passed away, leaving her as an orphan. Mordecai, her older cousin, took over the care of this poor waif. She was dependent upon him both financially and emotionally.

Through a series of remarkable events, Esther became Queen. She became independent of her cousin financially and could've easily disassociated from her family. They, likewise, could have abandoned her to the aristocracy and forgotten about her. Neither happened.

Mordecai continued to look out for Esther. He watched from afar, but she no longer relied on his presence with her. Instead, Mordecai needed Esther's help. He overheard a conspiracy to assassinate the King. In his lowly position he didn't have a way of communicating this to the King personally. Instead, he was humble enough to seek Esther's assistance. Imagine the consequences if he had proudly determined not to ask for help. History would've been written very differently.

Later, Mordecai found out that his cultural group

was about to be confronted with genocide. Esther, of course, also shared his cultural identity, but was blissfully unaware of the threat. She needed Mordecai to communicate the danger and ask for her help once more. Otherwise, she never would've known. Mordecai needed Esther to talk to the King to plead for her people.

Esther was aware that initiating conversation with the King could lead to her demise. She was probably scared. Yet she knew that she could depend on Mordecai. She humbled herself to ask Mordecai to gather prayer support. Then she also sought God for divine intervention.

Esther and Mordecai were interdependent. They could have chosen to work independently, but instead they relied on each other and on God. When we humble ourselves to ask for help, we can experience the blessing of receiving and give others the opportunity to participate in the blessing of giving.

"The Lord Jesus himself said: 'It is more blessed to give than to receive'" (Acts 20:35).

Giving is wonderful and we also need to give others the opportunity to give to us as well.

Let's make every day Interdependence Day... not Independence Day.

Further Reading: Matthew 7:7-12

Prayer: *Lord God, thanks for giving me so much. I am sorry for my pride at not asking for help. Please help me to share what I have with others as well as receiving from other people with gratitude.*
Amen

10

Two Men And Their Donkeys

There were two men with donkeys. The first man borrowed a colt that had never been ridden. The second man borrowed a donkey too. Both of them are remembered, years after their passing, because of their sacrifice, mateship and courage.

The first man rode a donkey into the capital city with a crowd of well-wishers. He was regaled as a King and acknowledged as the one who came in peace. He didn't ride a war horse, but the donkey showed the people that he came in peace.

The second man rescued wounded soldiers and carried them on the donkey. He didn't return fire as the bullets hailed around him, but rather he sought to bring some help and peace to people in pain. He courageously sought to be a mate to those who so desperately needed one.

The first man was also a mate to the sick and injured, but the people turned against him and called for blood. In the worst battle of all time, the first man courageously battled his demons. Because he sought to forge mateship between two parties at odds, he endured unspeakable atrocities. His sacrifice led to his death at an early age. He gave his life to save others.

The second man also risked his life to rescue others. When a bullet met its mark, Simpson passed away -

a hero to his mates. His legacy lives on as a selfless, courageous man.

The first man's legacy is even greater, because he died to bring peace to all nations. His brave endurance was for the sake of others. He sought to reconcile enemies and died in the process.

Jesus died, but it is not just His legacy that lives on, because He rose from the dead. He continues advocating for us.

"Greater love has no one than this: to lay down one's life for one's friends" (John 15:13).

Further Reading: John 12:12-35

Prayer: *Jesus, thanks for your great love for us, that you were willing to give your life for us. Thanks for your bravery and desire for peace and reconciliation. You are worthy of the highest honour.*
Amen

11

Light

The sun was retreating towards the horizon and the shadows were getting longer. Soon the inky darkness would descend like fog. How would they find their way?

One man took out his torch and flicked the on switch. A thin, barely perceptible, beam of light shone forth. He shook it a few times and the light went out altogether. Using only touch he pulled the torch apart and checked every link in the circuit. The bulb was fine and so was the connection between the conductors and the battery. Science could not help, however, when his battery was dead.

Another member of the party lit a match, but nearly burnt her fingers looking for something to light. As the flame brushed against her fingers she dropped the match, starting a small grass fire. Soon the tendrils of grass turned black, and wisps of smoke were the only reminder of that disastrous mistake. Playing with fire can be so dangerous.

A third girl found a candle stub and lit it with her lighter. She started down the winding path, but the people behind her couldn't see. She tried bending over backwards, but then she couldn't see. She tried holding the light up, but the chilling breeze licked at the flickering flame, threatening to blow it out. She shielded the light from the wind, but then she couldn't see in front of her. Suddenly a gust of wind whistled past her, extinguishing the wick. She had tried so hard to keep the path lit, using every good way she could think of.

Still the darkness crept in and tried to sap the warmth from their bodies.

A new guy approached them. They saw him coming because he had a light. He offered to let them follow him. At first they hesitated, but he reminded them that they would be in the dark soon if they didn't trust him, and they wouldn't be able to see where they were going. He raised his lantern up high and they looked up at the light. He started to continue his journey, and they hurriedly came to their senses and followed. They had to believe that the light was good for finding their way home.

Jesus said: "Believe in the light while you have the light, so that you may become children of light" (John 12:36).

Further Reading: John 12:44-50

Prayer: *God, you give us light to show us the way. Please give me light to help me to follow your way. Help me to trust you.*
Amen

12

It's NOT Fair!

It wasn't fair. He was stuck in a job he wouldn't have chosen for himself. He'd been forced into it by his brothers. Talk about drudgery! Joe had a choice to make. He could whine and complain, or he could ask God to help him do the best job he could. God was with him - even at work.

It wasn't fair. He'd been accused of sexual harassment, but he was innocent. The judge was biased, and Joe ended up thrown into prison. He had to make another decision. Would he mope about all day, or would he seek God's guidance to learn to deal with the situation? God was with him - even in the darkness.

It wasn't fair. He was hoping for release, but his case was forgotten. He'd cooperated with the authorities, and they repaid him by forgetting he even existed. Ranting and raving was an option, or he could turn his attention to prayer. God was with him - even when everyone else forgot he existed.

It wasn't fair. He was being summoned to court. At least they gave him time to shave and change his clothes. What was going on? A matter of high importance was at stake and Joe had been recognised as a necessary consultant. He knew he couldn't advise on such a matter, but he sought God to discern what to say.

It wasn't fair. He was being given a position far above his station. Joe was given a role he didn't deserve, but he recognised God's mercy in the situation. People in the past had sought to harm him, but Joe knew that God had used what was happening to help many people stay alive during a natural disaster. He didn't deserve to be honoured, but God was with him - whatever happened

"And we know that in all things God works for the good of those who love him, who have been called according to his purpose" (Romans 8:28).

Further Reading: Genesis 37; 39-45

Prayer: *Loving God, thanks that you walk beside your people. Thanks that you are with me at work, in difficult situations and even when I feel alone. Thanks that you are there in the good times and in the trials. Thanks that you can work all things for the good of those who love you. Lord, I have to say that I do complain when things don't seem to be going the way I want them to. Please help me to remember that you are there.*
Amen

13

Whatever It Takes

"I am not doing that!" The man was indignant. He had travelled from another country for this and for what? Nothing!

Who was this man? He was a high-ranking commanding officer who had huge responsibilities. He wasn't used to anyone telling him what to do. Usually, he was the one giving the orders. Even at home he had staff who did his domestic duties. They took care of the tasks at home so he could lead the forces at work.

This officer had a problem though. His health wasn't what it used to be. He had an irritating skin complaint that wouldn't go away and was potentially contagious. The medical professionals in his home country didn't have a treatment for it, but he desperately wanted his malady to go away.

Then he heard of a guy who might be able to help him. With a referral from a top ranking official, he packed his bags and headed off to see this foreigner. Once over the border, he headed straight for the government institution with high hopes that his mission would be successful. One look at his situation, however, left them tearing their hair out and wondering how to avoid a diplomatic catastrophe.

They had the officer transferred to a private place, but he was refused an audience with anyone who could help. Instead, a treatment plan was passed on by an unqualified employee who didn't know much about anything medical. The officer was enraged that these foreigners wouldn't even give him a consultation and his first inclination was to go home and ignore the advice given. It was too trivial to just go and have a wash!

The members of his party tried to reason with their commander. "If [he] had told you to do some great thing, would you not have done it? How much more, then, when he tells you, 'Wash and be cleansed!'" (2 Kings 5:13). Relenting, the officer followed the instructions and found that he had been healed. His actions were insignificant, but he ended up very grateful for a lovely, Divine blessing.

The man was so thankful, that he tried to pay the one who had given him the instructions, but the wise counsellor would not accept either money or clothes. How could he? The healing had been a gift from God.

Further Reading: 2 Kings 5

Prayer: *Almighty God, you are so much bigger than I am. Forgive me for my pride that wants to control what I will and won't do. Thank you that you have the power to help us, even when we think it is beneath us to ask. Lord, thanks for your encouragement to do things your way. Thanks for supplying me with what I need.*
Amen

14

Signs

It's a sign! Signs are everywhere. There are lots of them. Some are stop signs or ***do not _ _ _ _*** signs. Like the sign that says ***Danger! Crocodiles! Do not swim!*** We'd be crazy not to take notice of that sign. Then there are the ***No Food or Drink*** kind of signs that some people choose to ignore as mere suggestions. What do we do with the signs God gives? Do we take notice or ignore them?

Some signs say, ***Here it is!*** Toilet signs are like that. Some people can't go past a toilet without going in. The sign says the toilet is here. Shop signs are like that too. They say that herein lies a bakery, for example. If we read such a sign ***Bakery*** and walk in to find a blacksmith, it would be unusual to say the least. If we saw the sign ***Doctor*** and went in to find a mechanic, we would be wondering about the qualifications of the GP.

Jesus' signs indicated that He was God. There were no letters written in neon lights above His head or on a name badge. The signs were things that Jesus did... Awe inspiring acts of God that disrupted the course of nature... miracles. The signs showed the presence of the Kingdom of God. Where is the Kingdom of God? Jesus' signs said, ***Here it is.***

The Kingdom of God cannot be restricted to a place. Just as some signs give direction, like ***Emergency- turn***

right here, Jesus' signs give direction. Where do they point? Or maybe the question should be: WHO do they point to? They point to God. Like a ***One Way*** sign, Jesus shows us the signs that point to God. He, after all, is the ***one way*** to God and He has shown us the very nature of God.

God is not limited by space, time, or circumstances. He has power over all these things. God knows every concern that we have. How do we know? Jesus has shown us the signs.

Further Reading: John 4:46-54

*Prayer: **God thank you that Jesus has shown us signs that give us direction and help us to come towards you. Amen***

15

Burdens

The suitcase was heavy. The backpack weighed a tonne. It didn't help that I had a fractured right wrist and had to resort to using my weaker left hand to lift the burdens. What was in this baggage? It contained the essentials like clothes and food, but the needs of daily life could be burdensome. Day to day affairs could cause my shoulders to sag.

The weight of the load could wear me down. Just getting from the car to the check-in was enough to make me want to stop to rest, and lifting the thing onto the conveyor belt brought out a frown of consternation. At my destination there were stairs to go up, and my bag of boulders had to be heaved up each step.

When the bus driver lifted my burden and led the way to where I needed to go, I willingly followed. When he carried my load up the stairs, I was so grateful. By shouldering my burden, he lifted the weight off my back.

Jesus wants to trade the baggage of our daily lives for a bag ticket. He takes the weight of our lives, bound up by rules and regulations we can't keep, and replaces our burden with something that we can carry. By His grace He gives us relief and the weight of the world is taken into His hands. Then we can follow Him on the journey of life with freedom from the things that weigh us down. Thanks be to God.

Jesus said, "Come to me, all you who are weary and burdened, and I will give you rest" (Matthew 11:28).

Further reading: Matthew 11:28-30

Prayer: *Jesus, I have been trying to carry too much. I come to you. Please help me.*
Amen

16

Video Chat With God

Imagine two people having a video chat with God. One guy checks his appearance in the mirror before placing the call to God. He stands in front of his mobile, which is poised on a tripod. Lifting his eyes to heaven he raises his voice confidently:

"Thank you, God, that I am better than most people. I am in a position of authority where I can do my job well. Thank you that I am not a conman or a thief. I make time to pray regularly and give to charities."

What would God think of such a prayer?

Another bloke sits with his head in his hands. He doesn't even look at the camera. Mumbling, he pleads:

"God, I know I've done the wrong thing. I know I've done a lousy job of doing things the way you want. I'm sorry. Please have mercy on me. I don't deserve anything good God, but please don't reject me. I need your mercy."

What would God think of that prayer?

God wants us to connect with Him and we don't even need to have internet. Connection with God is wireless though! He appreciates our gratitude, our requests, and our apologies. What he doesn't like is self-righteousness, self-centredness, or self-aggrandisement.

"The Lord does not look at the things people look at. People look at the outward appearance, but the

Lord looks at the heart" (1 Samuel 16:7).

God knows exactly what we are like. Telling Him how wonderful we are will not earn any brownie points with Him. While He wants us to follow His ways, talk to Him, use our talents, and give generously, He doesn't need us to boast of our goodness or attempt to make ourselves look good. He would rather hear our honest confession that we know we've missed the mark.

Further reading: Luke 18:9-14

Prayer: *God, please help me to be real with you. Nothing I can do can make you love me more, and nothing I do wrong stops you from loving me. I know I've done things I shouldn't have done. There's no point in trying to justify anything to you because you know my motives. Help me to stop doing things my own way. Help me instead to go your way.*
Amen

17

Easter Re-enactment

I wanted a main role, but they had all been filled. The director asked me to make myself known at the first rehearsal so he could put me in charge of part of the crowd. When I got to the rehearsal, there were people everywhere. My confidence disappeared and I melted into the crowd. There was no way I could lead all these people. I had tried to exalt myself, under the guise of wanting to use the talents God had given me. Instead, I was humbled. I used my talents to help two younger girls develop their characters for the Easter re-enactment instead.

How different was Jesus' attitude. He didn't seek the top job... I mean you can't get higher than God. Rather He sought to obey the Father; even to the point of pain... lots of pain. He wasn't about exalting Himself or getting attention. He was humble. It wasn't until the Father exalted Him that Jesus regained equality with God.

Being part of the Easter re-enactment was an amazing experience. Hearing crowds of people singing and dancing as Jesus entered Jerusalem was moving. The atmosphere was electric. Then to be part of an equally passionate crowd shouting, "Crucify Him!" brought the reality of Jesus' predicament into sharp focus. The anger and rage stirred up by the religious leaders created a mob mentality. Jesus could've called down angels to free Him from that hate fest. But He didn't. He could've called down fire to destroy those godless people, but instead He endured their wrath. He was humble to the end.

"And being found in appearance as a man, he humbled himself by becoming obedient to death— even death on a cross!" (Philippians 2:8).

I wonder what impact the Easter re-enactment had on the audience. I hope they had a sense of Jesus' humble meekness - harnessed strength. I also hope that they were moved to tears at the immensity of Jesus' love for them... that He would be willing to go through all that He did, because of love.

Further Reading: Philippians 2:5-11

Prayer: *Jesus thank you for being so humble that you would willingly allow people to put you on a cross to die. Thank you that you came back to life and have been exalted to the highest place now.*
Amen

18

Hail

A noisy cacophony of sound poured from the heavens to the ground. Hail stones bounced off the carport and the grass alike. My car was in the garage, so I was enjoying watching this stormy spectacle. Cars were stopping on the road near our driveway. We had space in the carport. I had to help someone get out of the storm. Braving the pelting balls of ice, I rushed out to the road and gestured for a car to come up the drive, and then I bolted for cover. My hand was a poor crash helmet, but at least it stopped the full impact of the hail from beating against my skull. Soaked to the skin, I was freezing cold, so I quickly found shelter in the warm house.

Hail has often fascinated me. I remember picking up "snow" (hail) off the front lawn. I missed that deluge, but the ice was still there when I arrived. It was like a thick blanket, and it had come with such power. I have lots of questions about hail that are as yet unanswered. Why does the sky turn green before a hailstorm? Why do these icy cold hailstones often fall in summer? Some things may never make sense to me.

God is also fascinating. I have many questions about Him too! He is more powerful than a hailstorm, more glorious than lightning, and more puzzling than green clouds. He is surrounded by both mystery and majesty and what's more amazing is that He lets us glimpse His awesomeness from time to time. How great He is!

"Praise the Lord. Praise the Lord from the heavens; praise him in the heights above" (Psalm 148:1).

Further Reading: Psalm 148

Prayer: *God you are awesome. You are powerful, glorious and beyond our understanding. Thank you for giving us a glimpse of how wonderful you are. Amen*

19

Pure Gold

Have you ever owned a gold watch? Was it pure gold? Precious metals often have other minerals mixed with them. I believe that gold is refined and purified using high temperatures. When the heat is turned up, the impurities can be removed. This process can be repeated until the gold is so pure that the goldsmith can see their reflection mirrored in the gold.

It is a compliment to hear the words: "You have a heart of gold." I wonder how this saying originated. Is the metaphor talking about someone being soft hearted, being of great value, or being pure like refined gold? Maybe it is talking about all three ideas... or something else entirely. The purer gold is, the more valuable it becomes, so maybe the ideas are linked.

Pure gold is also rare and during a drought in the bush, water has been called liquid gold. It is rare, highly valuable and costs a huge amount to buy. Service stations in the outback don't give out cups of water for free when they have to pay exorbitant prices to have water shipped out to them. Bottled water also costs money. I'd rather pay a fortune for water I knew was pure enough to drink, than try to boil or purify water found in the bush. I would probably die of thirst before I could find any liquid gold in the outback as my bush survival skills are not that well-honed.

Even though my bushcraft is a bit rusty, I enjoy being in the bush. I used to love going to Crystal Creek as a child. The water was cool and clear. I considered it pure. Unfortunately, not all impurities are visible, so I could have been drinking contaminated water, for all I knew. Pure water has not been compromised with germs, chemicals, or other additives. Similarly, pure lives don't compromise with temptation or have mixed motives. "All a person's ways seem pure to them, but motives are weighed by the Lord" (Proverbs 16:2).

When pure rainwater falls in a rainforest it can make the ferns sparkle. It is liquid gold, adorning the greenery with jewellery. I want to be like that... adorned with purity, such that I sparkle and reflect the image of the Goldsmith who continues to purify my heart until I have a heart of pure gold.

Further Reading: Psalm 19

Prayer: *Lord you are completely pure. You know my thoughts and motives. Lord, please forgive me for my impure motives and purify my heart until you can clearly see your reflection in my heart of gold.*
Amen

20

Who Is This Guy?

Who do you say that Jesus is?

Some people thought Jesus was really a guy named John. John called a spade a spade and was known for his truthfulness. During his life John called people to stop doing things their own way and to follow God's way. He was a great moral teacher. Jesus also called people to uphold the moral code. He taught people to "Love the Lord your God with all your heart and with all your soul and with all your mind and with all your strength," and to "Love your neighbor as yourself" (Mark 12:30-31). Do you see Jesus as a great moral teacher?

Other people around during Jesus' ministry thought Jesus was a man named Elijah. Why? What was significant about Elijah? Elijah had great courage and challenged people to make a choice between following God or not. Elijah's calling was accompanied by supernatural signs. Jesus' ministry was also characterised by a call to only serve one master... the living God, and He showed God's power through supernatural signs and wonders. Do you see Jesus as a miracle worker?

There were also some contemporaries of Jesus who saw Jesus as a prophet. Jesus spoke with authority that came from God and He did what prophets did... He gave messages to the people from God. He knew things that one could only know if God revealed them. Jesus also foretold events that were yet to come, such as the destruction of the temple in Jerusalem. In this way Jesus was like Jeremiah who foretold judgment, but also spoke of hope in the Lord. Do you see Jesus as a prophet?

Peter saw Jesus as the Messiah, God's chosen King. The Israelites had been awaiting a Messiah for a very long time. Many people had a distorted view of the Messiah though, hoping that He would drive out their oppressors from Rome. He was to be a political hero. Instead, Jesus came as God's chosen one to bring the Kingdom of God near. Do you see Jesus as the Messiah?

Peter also considered Jesus to be the Son of the Living God. He didn't see Jesus as a prophet or an idol... a lifeless 'god'. He perceived that Jesus was connected to the real, living, and active God of the universe. Peter saw that Jesus was related in an intimate way with God the Father. They were as close as a Father and Son could ever be. Do you see Jesus as the Son of God?

Who do you say Jesus is? Why?

Further Reading: Matthew 16:13-17

Prayer: *God show me more of who you are. Help me to know, not just about you, but to know you as a friend. I don't know if anyone understands you fully or how you can be Father, Son, and Spirit, but help me to see you more clearly.*
Amen

21

Noble Service

The carriage pulled to a stop outside the stables. The Duke and Duchess shuffled nervously. What was taking James so long? They were at the head of an entourage of Earls, Countesses, and Dukes. The Duke poked his head out of the covered carriage. The stable doors were closed.

Without hesitation, the Duke leapt to the ground and drew back the heavy bolts holding the doors in place. Going in ahead of his chauffeur, he saw his head stable-hand lying unconscious in one of the empty stalls. "James!" he cried. Blood crusted on the man's temple. "Call for a doctor!" he called to his driver, as he knelt in the straw. Quickly shaking the man, the Duke was given a murmur in reply. Taking a handkerchief from his breast pocket, he wet it under a nearby tap and gently washed the wounded man's brow.

"I say Duke, what's the hold up old chap?" came an Earl's impatient voice from near the entrance. Quickly the Duchess alighted from her carriage and spoke in soft tones to the frustrated guest. She led her horses forward in the royal stable and gently patted the stallion's shoulder. "I'll be back boy," the Duchess whispered in his ear.

Then lifting her ballgown with grace and poise, she led each carriage into the grounds, assisted the guests to alight and escorted the steeds back to their shelter for the night. "Haven't you got servants to handle that?" a dear Countess asked with a plumb in her mouth. Eloquently, the Duchess replied that she had dismissed them for the evening in order to have the privilege of serving her guests herself. "Oh, but my dear," the Countess countered, "it's unheard of for a Duchess to muddy one's heels amongst the manure. I simply cannot condone it. Please send for a valet or I shall not alight."

"If I can't have the privilege of serving you my dear, then I am afraid I can no longer welcome you as a guest. Please let me assist you into the drawing room, or I fear I will need to ask your driver to return you to your estate." Humbled by the Duchesses' grace and care, the Countess stepped gingerly down from where she could look down on the world and followed this courageous royal into the palace.

Moments later, the Duchess descended the steps once more to stable the horses, before welcoming the next guests.

Further reading: John 13:1-17

Prayer: *Noble Lord, thanks that you in all your greatness willingly took on the role of a servant to be the servant King. Thank you for giving us the example of how to be a servant leader and how to love.*
Amen

22

The Return

The roar of the wheels hitting the tarmac reminded him of how far he had fallen. As he went out of the airport doors, he wondered what to do. He had no money, and it was his own fault. Taxis and public transport were out, so he'd have to walk, but where would he go? He started to walk, having no idea where he was going. As he trudged along the side of the road, his nose began to twitch. What was that stench? The curbs were coated in brown sludge, and even the grass and trees had turned a dirty brown colour. As he got to the first house the landscape changed. There were piles and piles of rubbish on the street.

When darkness started to dim his surroundings, he began to look for a place to sleep. Hunger gnawed at him as he decided to take shelter under one of the stinking piles of junk. There was a mattress… he crawled in and burst back out again. Mould was already growing thick, and the stench was unbearable on the soggy mess of mattress. A little further down the street he found half a rotten apple covered in silt. Hungrily he devoured what was left of the apple including the core, trying hard not to gag. Looking around he decided that the gutter was the best place to sleep. Oh, how far he had fallen.

It hadn't always been like this. He had grown up

in a tropical fruit orchard, lush with healthy green vegetation. His dad owned the plantation and he and his brother had helped to manage the property. But then he'd got itchy feet and had wanted more. Discontented, he had asked his dad to pay up his share and then taken off for fairer lands. It wasn't long before he built up a reputation of his own, but not the kind of reputation his kind, generous dad would be pleased with. That's when he spent everything he had and was deported back to his country of origin.

What was he going to do now? About midnight, thunder started to growl, and rain began pouring down in torrents. It was right about then that he made a decision. Even his father's fruit pickers lived better than this. He decided to go home, eat humble pie, and ask his dad for a job, despite the fact that he didn't deserve one. Drenched to the bone, he started on the long road home.

When he came to the entrance of his dad's property, he saw someone running towards him. He was almost ready to bolt, but he didn't have the energy. Then he realised it was his dad coming to enfold him in a big hug. There would be a welcome home party, the dad explained to his staff.

"For this son of mine was dead and is alive again; he was lost and is found. So they began to celebrate" (Luke 15:24).

Further reading: Luke 15:11-32

Prayer: *Father God, thank you that you are kind and generous like that dad. I am sorry I have gone my own way, instead of your way. Please forgive me and help me to know what it's like to be a part of your great family.*
Amen

23
Complaints Or Compliments

"I liked it better the old way!" "I've had enough of this! I'm leaving." "When is this ever going to end?" "I'm so bored." "Not again!" "I'm over this." "We were better off the way it was before."

The people were good at complaining. They complained about not having enough food, having too much food, the type of food, the leadership, the lack of water, the location of their accommodation, their living conditions, their potential neighbours, their future prospects. You name it - they complained about it.

Before we write them off as ungrateful so and sos, what's our own self talk like? "I'm sick of this." "I've had chicken coming out of my ears." "I wish I could have a roast." "I don't want to do that." "What are those leaders doing?" "That's not the way he should be doing things." "Why can't we go back to doing things the way they were?" Do we grumble about things too?

The people had God's presence with them. They had a column of cloud to guide them by day and fire by night. It was more than their own personal GPS. They had clear direction from God. This is the same God who had miraculously released them from slavery and then parted the Red Sea, just so they could escape from the Egyptian army. It is also the same God who provided them with manna, quail, and essential water in an unforgiving desert. It was a miracle.

We have even more opportunities than them. God's guidance is near to those who call on Him. He wants to deliver us from slavery to our self-centredness. Jesus has miraculously risen from the dead, so that we might have eternal life if we choose to trust Him. This God gives us food to eat, work to do, water to drink and meets all our needs.

Let's see if we can change our complaints to compliments of God's goodness. What would it hurt to "Give thanks in all circumstances"? (1 Thessalonians 5:18).

Further reading: Numbers 20:1-11

Prayer: *Lord thanks that you give so many good things to me. Thanks for running water, food to eat, air to breathe and for everything else you grant me. I'm sorry I complain. Help me to appreciate your goodness.*
Amen

24
Climbing The Ladder

He'd done it! He'd finally done it!

As a child, the teachers used to tell him that he'd never amount to anything. Well now he could prove them wrong. It hadn't started off very easy. His first job had been sorting garbage. The school of hard knocks taught him that it was a nightmare going through other people's rubbish. He would go home after each shift stinking like a sewer rat.

Every pay he put aside ten measly cents. It wasn't much and there were times that he could've used that money. Instead, he disciplined himself to save it. When he had enough accumulated, he invested in the stock market. It took him years of scrimping and saving, with much personal sacrifice, before he felt like he'd begun to climb out of the garbage.

Now, after climbing the corporate ladder rung-by-rung for years, he had made more than enough to live on. He had already purchased a big house, a fast car, more toys than his 2.5 kids could ever want, and a ring for his wife. He hoped showering his family with things would help make up for the time he never spent with them.

He considered his options. Should he buy a bigger house, travel the world, or maybe become part owner of a yacht? Finally, he decided to cash in all his shares and reinvest his money. Then he decided that early retirement was the way to go, where he could wine and dine in luxury for the rest of his life. He could lie back, put his feet up and enjoy himself.

Little did he know that he would pass away that very night.

"This is how it will be with whoever stores up things for themselves but is not rich toward God" (Luke 12:21).

Further reading: Luke 12:13-21

Prayer: *Generous God, thank you for providing for my needs over the years. Forgive me for when I have stored up things for myself without considering what you want me to do with the resources. Please help me not to try to buy my way into heaven (as that is impossible), but to use what I have to be a blessing. Please help me to take time to invest in the lives of the people around me, not to earn my way into heaven (as that is again impossible), but to bless them.*
Amen

25

The Lifesaver

Gurgle gurgle. Splash. Silence. Splash. Gasp! "Help!" He was drowning and although he tried to fight it, each movement made him weaker and weaker. After the gasp, sucking in life-giving air, he began to sink below the waves. Down, down, down. Then a shadow passed in front of the sun. A hand reached toward the drowning man, and he weakly reached up but couldn't touch the hand. The rescuer reached down further and hauled him onto the rescue boat. Then everything went black.

"There's no breathing!" "Base this is rescue boat 001. We've got a near drowning with no breathing. Please contact emergency services." "Check the airway." "Clear. I will start CPR." "1, 2, 3... 30. Breathe. Breathe. 1, 2..." As the boat made its way back through the pounding surf, the lifesaver continued to breathe into the guy's lungs. Would he be able to save this guy's life?

Crashing into the beach, the rescue team jumped out and dragged the boat up onto the sand. The lifesaver doing CPR kept going, even though he was beginning to fatigue. This guy's life depended on it. Sirens approached from the road. "1, 2... 27." **Splutter, cough.** "He's breathing!"

What if he had died? Where would he have spent eternity? I guess it depends on who he trusted. It's not what you know... it's who you know. If he trusted Jesus, then he would be able to spend eternity in the best place ever. If he didn't, then he would suffer forever. He needed someone to save his life... and his eternal life.

"If you declare with your mouth, 'Jesus is Lord', and believe in your heart that God raised him from the dead, you will be saved" (Romans 10:9). This survivor of near drowning was resuscitated. Jesus wasn't. He was fully dead and was raised back to being fully alive. He is the only eternal Lifesaver able to save us from suffering that goes on forever.

Further Reading: Acts 16:16-34

Prayer: *Lord Jesus, I believe you are alive and can be my eternal Lifesaver. I trust you to rescue me from a fate worse than death. Jesus, Son of God, thanks for dying and coming back to life because it gives me hope that you can save my eternal life. Jesus you are Lord. Forgive me for doing things my way and not your way. Help me to live your way forever with you.*
Amen

26

Greatness

From the beach to the rainforest, from the sand to the sky, there are whispers and shouts of greatness. There it is again… a whisper in the wind. A ripple on the water, a footprint in the sand, and a feather in the branches all give clues to a great mystery. What is this greatness they speak of?

Kookaburras laugh joyfully, while whipbirds call and swallows glide. Kingfishers watch and honeyeaters flit from bloom to bloom. All declare the greatness of God. He is their creator, and He has created them in beautiful splendour. We can give thanks that God has such an amazing imagination and awesome creativity.

A soldier crab tries to bury itself into the hand that holds it, seeking protection from danger. God too wants to hold us in His comforting protection. His steadfast love endures forever, and His compassion is unfailing, so we can bury ourselves in His unconditional love, knowing that He is kind.

A tiny snail tentatively extends its tentacle out of its shell into the shallow water around it. As it comes out of its shell it is vulnerable. God has created in intricate detail and knows where the vulnerabilities hide. With great tenderness, He extends His goodness to the tiniest of creatures. His gentleness to the fragile is beyond compare.

Pure water bubbles up from the sand. It cannot contain itself, but must burst forth and flow in gentle currents, testifying to the restrained power of the Lord God almighty. His is a power that can make everything from nothing with a word.

The stars burn brightly, testifying to the explosive power of our Great God. The Southern Cross stands out, declaring the praises of the One who once suffered on a cross, but was raised again to life with the same power that makes the stars explode with such intensity that their light can be seen light years away.

"Great is the Lord and most worthy of praise; his greatness no one can fathom" (Psalm 145:3).

Further Reading: Psalm 145

Prayer: *Great and mighty God you are so good. Your greatness is far beyond what we can imagine. You are slow to anger and abounding in love. You are more powerful than a shooting star and gentler than a quiet breeze.*
Amen

27
The Ransom

Gagged and tied to a chair, the hostage looked around like a scared rabbit. Was she about to die? Her kidnapper turned around with a knife clutched in his hand. With eyes like saucers, she made whimpers of protest. She didn't want to die. She closed her eyes in terror.

The kidnapper moved quickly. Seconds later it was all over. She tentatively opened her eyes. Her bonds had been cut and her gag removed. "Don't try to scream. No one will ever hear you," snarled her captor.

"Look I can pay you whatever you want, just let me go," she pleaded. "No can do," replied the kidnapper casually. "Ransom for your life is higher than anyone could pay me."

Looking around the room, she spotted a sink stacked with grimy dishes, a floor littered with rubbish and a toilet tinged with brown. Thinking quickly, she headed for the sink. "What are you doing?" asked the guy, alert for any tricks. "I thought I would give you a hand to clean up," replied the woman. "That won't change my mind. I ain't letting you go, no matter how much stuff you do." Deflated, she did the dishes anyway. At least then her captor couldn't see her desperate expression.

Knock, **knock**, **knock**, came from the door. "Who are you and what do you want?" demanded the kidnapper warily. "My name isn't important, but you have my daughter." Quickly the kidnapper poked a knife under the woman's chin, warning her not to say a word. The man at the door continued, "I have come to negotiate with you. I want to propose a swap. Would you consider taking me as a hostage and letting my daughter go free?"

Jesus "did not come to be served, but to serve, and to give his life as a ransom for many" (Mark 10:45).

Further Reading: Matthew 20:20-28

Prayer: *Lord Jesus, thank you that you came to serve and give your life of your own free will. Jesus, thanks for putting your life on the line in order to offer me my freedom. I don't deserve your help. I have been proud of my own feeble efforts to help others, but you did even more to help me. Please help me to appreciate the fullness of your ransom.*
Amen

28
Will It Ever End?

Creak, groan, oof! are the familiar sounds of my body getting out of a chair. Doctor's appointments, specialist appointments, pathology, X-rays, scans, ultrasounds, pills, exercises, and painkillers seem to be unending. Then there's the emotional pain of watching loved ones repeatedly getting hurt or hurting others. Families can be so mixed up and where's the loyalty of friends these days? Then there are the atrocities people around the world commit against each other. What is the world coming to? We shake our heads at the latest act of cruelty broadcast around the world. Will it ever end?

What would it look like if our dreams were to come true? There would be no more sickness, pain or dying in my ideal picture. Poverty would no longer exist, and wars would no longer happen. There would be global peace. Domestic violence, child abuse and malicious gossip would all be eliminated. Children would no longer lie point blank to their teachers, and price gouging would be a distant memory. Floods and looting after disasters would be no more.

Love would trump hate; consideration would win over selfishness; truth would replace conspiracy and lies; and good would triumph over evil. Everyone would look out for their neighbour to see how they could make their day. Relationships would always be loving, genuine and pure. Joy and peace would be the norm. Sounds heavenly to me!

One day I hope to see a new heaven and new earth where "There will be no more death or mourning or crying or pain" (Revelation 21:3-4).

How do I know if I will get to experience this?

There must be a way to experience heaven. I have to find out what it is.

Further Reading: Revelation 21

Prayer: *God there's so much suffering in the world that I don't understand. Please help those who are in pain. Thanks that you will recreate heaven and earth where there won't be any more pain. Please help me to know how to get to heaven.*
Amen

29

The Good Neighbour

*B*ang! A 4x4 rammed into a sedan stopped at the lights. The driver of the sedan was stunned. Seconds later a fist was thrust through the window as the perpetrator set about beating his victim into unconsciousness. Slumped over the steering wheel, this recipient of road rage looked like death warmed up.

Headed up the road came a local elder. At first the elder waited patiently for the light to turn green, but then realised that the traffic still wasn't moving and started to honk his horn. He was late for an important meeting. Sometime later he realised that the driver in front was slumped over the wheel. Muttering something about drunk drivers, the elder indicated and changed lanes to give the car a wide berth.

A short time later, one of the ladies from a local charity ended up behind the injured driver. She noticed that the car had been damaged and checked her watch. She didn't have time to get involved. Besides, the driver was probably on drugs anyway. Making a quick decision she skirted around the car and sped off to deliver bread to a needy family.

After a few minutes a young guy with ripped jeans, a nose ring, tattoos, and dreadlocks pulled up behind the sedan on his motorbike. He turned off his bike and went over to the driver side window. "Hey man what's up?" asked the youth. When the victim didn't reply, he whipped out his mobile phone and called for an ambulance. He noticed there was bleeding, so he took off his bandana and tried to stop the flow of blood. When the ambulance arrived, the youth moved his bike onto the nature strip and jumped in the ambulance alongside the victim. When asked if he was family he said "nah, but this one might need a mate down the track," so the ambos said he could stay.

Later in the day the victim regained consciousness. Right beside the bed was the bikie asking if there was anything else that was needed.

"Which of these three do you think was a neighbor to the man...?" (Luke 10:36).

Further reading: Luke 10:25-37

Prayer: *Merciful God help me to love you, and others, like you love me. I know I don't always show kindness and I may be hypocritical at times too. I know I am not perfect. Please forgive me and help me to match my words and actions.*
Amen

30

The Royal Wedding

The Royal Family were preparing a royal wedding… well actually their servants were doing most of the work. The silver had to be polished, the grounds had to be immaculate, and the royal carriage needed to gleam. Then there were the invitations to send and banquet food to order and prepare.

As money was no object, all the courtiers were invited. Dukes, Duchesses, Earls, Countesses, Admirals, Generals, Princes, and Princesses were among the nobles on the royal guest list. The privileged aristocracy were indeed privileged to receive an invitation.

On the date of the RSVP, a royal courier was dispatched to collect confirmation of these nobles' attendance. He was greeted at the door of the first palace by the resident butler. Instead of being invited to wait in the drawing room, the courier was left to wait at the door. He wasn't greeted by the Duke himself, but the butler soon returned.

"Please convey to your majesty that the Duke will be unable to attend the wedding celebrations as he has just acquired a new estate and needs to make a thorough inspection of the property."

The courier made a note on his royal guest list and proceeded to the next guest on his parchment. Approaching the front entrance, he was greeted again by a butler. This one curtly apologised for his Countess, who herself had been pledged to be married on the same day as the royal wedding. She was preparing to be married to a man of noble birth and was very much looking forward to the coming alliance.

Next, the courier sought the audience of an admiral. Instead, an able seaman passed the courier a letter bearing the admiral's seal. It read: "Your Royal Highness, I regret to inform you that I will be unable to attend the royal wedding as I have recently been given command of a fleet of battleships, and I am obliged to oversee their departures."

Discouraged by repeated rejections, the courier trudged back to the castle. He reported to the Sovereign that not one of his dignitaries were planning to attend the royal festivities. Turning a shade of scarlet, the King decreed that not one of the nobles invited deserved to come because they sought to be rulers of their own destinies. Instead, the common folk, who appreciated the reign of the royals, were to be invited. Anyone who was willing to accept the King's generosity, would be welcomed into the ballroom. It didn't matter if they didn't have anything appropriate to wear as they would be given suitable garments, fitting to the occasion.

When the wedding day arrived, there was much pomp and ceremony. One man, however, didn't feel right about wearing the King's finery. He was too proud to accept charity and refused to change his clothes, even though they were filthy and tattered. He soon came to the notice of the King, who was disappointed that the man wouldn't accept his gifts. Guards escorted the man from the premises. Meanwhile the poor, the blind, and the crippled all enjoyed the lavish banquet and the overwhelming generosity of the King.

"The kingdom of heaven is like a king who prepared a wedding banquet for his son" (Matthew 22:2).

Further reading: Matthew 22:1-14

Prayer: *God, you are the King of Kings. Forgive me for when I am proud or just want to do things my own way. Please help me to humbly accept the gifts you offer.*
Amen

31

Citizenship

Becoming a citizen of Australia is a big deal. It requires patience, commitment, and hard work. It also costs money, but the biggest cost is in the sweat and tears it takes to become proficient at English. The language demands are hard for native speakers of English, let alone those wanting to migrate here. The standard is very high. It's a great deal easier to be born in Australia or to have Australian parents.

Becoming a citizen of heaven is also a big deal... bigger than changing where we live. We can't be born citizens of heaven and our parents' citizenship can't help us. Each person has to become a citizen personally. The standard is perfection. It is impossible to manipulate the system with pretence because hypocrisy is easily detected. Neither can we earn our way through hard work or pay with money.

We need an ambassador to help us to become citizens of heaven. We need someone who meets the standard of perfection to make up for our imperfections. He isn't an immigration officer who works through the red tape. There is no red tape. He is the ambassador himself, representing the Monarch, while also being royalty. Only He has the power and authority to grant us citizenship of heaven. We can't go to the court of appeals above Him because He has the highest authority.

Fortunately for us our ambassador is merciful. He delights in granting citizenship. There is no rubber stamp that says 'accepted' because there are no forms to fill in. We apply for citizenship by asking the ambassador to be our saviour and allowing Him to lead us in the way we should go. Jesus is our ambassador. He has the highest authority, because God the Father exalted Him when Jesus submitted to death and then came back to life. Jesus said, "Whoever comes to me I will never drive away" (John 6:37). That means if we are willing to come to Jesus, we can apply for citizenship to heaven without fear.

When we are granted citizenship to heaven our perspective changes. We may face enemies, but our passport is hidden in our heart, and nobody can steal it. We are accepted and we belong with Jesus.

Further Reading: Philippians 3:17-4:1

Prayer: *Jesus thank you for being a merciful ambassador. Thanks that you desire to help us to become citizens of heaven. Help me to know how I can be a citizen of heaven.*
Amen

A note to the reader

God is thinking of you. What do you think of Him? Are you ready to say you believe God is real? Are you at the point of wanting to start a friendship with God? If you still have questions, then I would encourage you to seek out the answers until you find them. If you want to start a new friendship with God, then read on.

God loves you so much that He sent His Son Jesus, who was fully God and fully human, to earth. Jesus lived a perfect life, but the authorities of His day didn't believe He was the Son of God.

They arranged to have Jesus put to death on a cross. Jesus could've stopped it, but He didn't, because He was thinking of God the Father, and He was thinking of you. Jesus knew that His death was the only way that you could be friends with God. No matter how thoughtful we are or how much we do that is considered good by those around us, God knows that we have gone our own way, not His way. That has caused a major rift between us and God. Only Jesus' death to pay the penalty for our guilt can lead to a reconciliation between us. Jesus didn't stay dead though. He came back to life, showing that He was fair dinkum about who He was. The Bible tells us that

He is more than thinking of you... He's advocating for you. The question is: are you ready to call Jesus your best friend? Are you ready to become a citizen of heaven?

If the answer is yes, then here is a prayer you can pray:

Thank you, God, that Jesus, the Son of God, came to live as a man on earth. I am sorry I have not lived a perfect life like Jesus did. Please forgive me. Thanks that Jesus died so that I can be friends with you God. Thanks that Jesus is alive again. I invite you to be my eternal Lifesaver and Lord, Jesus. God, please come into my life and help me to live your way. Amen.

If you prayed this prayer, sincerely believing it, then I would encourage you to keep talking to God every day and read His love letter to you - the Bible. Tell someone about your new friendship with God, but don't be surprised if they don't get it. It would also be wise for you to find a Christian church where you can be encouraged in your relationship with God.

Thinking of you.

Donna Turnbull

Acknowledgements

I want to thank my parents, Elaine and Bruce, for their part in helping me to reach the dream of publishing this book. Without them, this opportunity would've been beyond me.

I am also very grateful to my friend, Linda Watt. She has been a mega blessing to me as we have navigated the complexities of publication.

I am grateful to the photographers and artists who have helped bring beauty to compliment what has been written. All internal images have been sourced from Pixabay.

Most of all I would like to thank God for equipping me to write this book and providing me with the necessary resources. To God be the glory.

www.ingramcontent.com/pod-product-compliance
Lightning Source LLC
Chambersburg PA
CBHW051539010526
44107CB00064B/2781